CONTENTS

✦ INTRODUCTION ✦

Have you ever met a stranger and felt you were fated to be friends? Or set eyes on your date and bristled at the vibes – even before they've uttered a word?

You may have answered yes to these questions, but have you ever stopped to question the source of these powerful intuitions? It might be that you're already more attuned to the hidden world of auras than you know.

Everyone has an aura. A shimmering, technicolour halo of light and energy, as unique as a fingerprint. The ever-shifting shades of your aura can reveal everything there is to know about your physical and emotional state.

Catching a glimpse of your own aura can be a magical, empowering experience, allowing you to take control of your well-being and relationships. This book aims to provide you with the knowledge and confidence you'll need to do exactly that. As you explore its pages, you'll learn about the layers of auras and how they fit into the ancient doctrine of Buddhism. You will also find practical tips to help you forge more meaningful relationships, both professional and personal, and you'll learn how to cleanse your aura to become a healthier, happier version of your wonderful self.

WHAT ARE AURAS?

Even if you class yourself as a complete novice, who's never glimpsed the faintest glow of spiritual energy around anyone, chances are you already have some understanding of the term "aura". Whether you're blasting Taylor Swift's "Bejeweled" or browsing Gwyneth Paltrow's Goop blog, auras are all-pervasive in popular culture. Yet the cultural roots of the aura go much deeper. From the Buddhists of the ancient world to the theosophists of the 1900s, auras have sparked the imagination of generations of thinkers, writers and scientists across the globe. This chapter delves into their full, fascinating history to give you a deeper understanding of what auras are truly made of.

✦ MIRROR FOR THE SOUL ✦

It's easy to point to the physical body. The face you can see staring back at you in the mirror. The skin that you can touch. The voice that speaks your thoughts out loud. But there's so much more that makes you *you*.

You can hide your emotions behind a poker face and keep your true thoughts to yourself while making idle chat. But, as the saying goes, the vibes don't lie. And neither does your auric energy, which will always be the first, most crucial part of yourself that you share with the world. For this reason, the aura is often associated with the "subtle body": a profoundly spiritual part of your being that can't be seen, only felt.

An aura is the field of electromagnetic energy that surrounds every living thing. Person, pet or houseplant, you're sure to be emitting one. Despite our differences, we are all made of energy. We absorb it and we release it, flooding the space around us with our own uniquely beautiful frequencies.

It's a never-ending cycle, as natural as breathing. Still, it pays to be mindful of the vibes we're sending out. An aura is the closest thing we have to a mirror for the soul, reflecting our thoughts and emotions.

Because energy speaks to energy, our auras can be a powerful force in shaping relationships. Finding friends you instantly "vibe" with has everything to do with the energy you're putting out and how it resonates with others. Your aura can be your siren song or a deafening alarm. So, if you want to change up your inner circle, start by taking stock of your own auric health.

✦ NOW YOU SEE ME... ✦

If auras are so common, you might be wondering why you haven't seen one. Few people are lucky enough to be born clairvoyant, with the gift of seeing energies.

Children are far more open to seeing auric energy than adults. But it's a skill they often unlearn – thanks to the grown-ups in their lives, who can be all too ready to dismiss their kids' visions as the products of a vivid imagination.

Even if you're not a natural, you shouldn't lose hope of ever glimpsing an auric glow. Anyone can choose to open their mind – and their eyes – to the beautiful world of auras. All it takes is practice, using techniques which we'll explore later in this book.

Even in the unlikely event that you never see an aura, feeling the quality of these energies (a great strength of clairsentient people) can prove just as enlightening.

THE AURA GIVEN OUT
BY A PERSON OR OBJECT
IS AS MUCH A PART OF
THEM AS THEIR FLESH.

LUCIEN FREUD

✦ THE UNIVERSE OF YOU ✦

Your aura is anything but two-dimensional. It surrounds your body in a shimmering haze of energy and light. Like a protective shield you never knew you had, it is to your body what ozone is to the Earth. From head to toe, it encircles every inch of you to form a rainbow-hued bubble of energy.

Auras mostly extend two to three feet beyond our bodies. But that can change in a heartbeat. When we're feeling sociable and electric, our energy can expand to fill a room, encompassing everyone within a 20-foot radius. In more introverted moments, it can shrink to next to nothing, clinging to us like a second skin.

Like an actual rainbow, every aura can be broken down into seven layers, which we'll explore in the next chapter. Each is a crucial part of the picture, expressing something unique about your inner state. Together, they form a whole that's as intricate as the universe of thought and emotion that exists inside of you.

IN THE LAND OF
GODS AND MONSTERS

Even the word "aura" has its own poetic backstory. Before it was an energy field or even a more general term for the unique atmosphere surrounding a person or a place, Aura was the name of a beautiful nymph in Greek mythology. She was the daughter of a Titan god, Lelantos, the god of the air. Thanks to her lofty parentage, her name will always be synonymous with breaths of gentle breeze – the fresh, healing winds that blow in with each new morning. Is there any more evocative way to conjure up the feeling you get when you meet another person vibrating on exactly the frequency you were hoping to find – a kindred spirit whose cool, cleansed aura aligns so perfectly with your own?

Having such a heightened awareness of your own auric energy, and the energies of those around you, can feel like the sun coming up on a thrilling new day.

✦ A BRIEF HISTORY OF AURAS ✦

Trace the cultural roots of the aura back through time and there's no telling where the search will take you. The aura is a concept that's travelled through centuries and across continents, to the endless fascination of savants, philosophers and scientists everywhere.

The aura holds a special place in ancient Egyptian mythology, under the name of "ka", the life force that links us with the divine. In Greek, this concept translates as "pneuma", invisible breaths of life-giving energy that make us who we are.

In sacred Christian spaces, no depiction of Jesus or the angels would be complete without a halo, a symbol of inner-goodness and enlightenment worn like a luminous gold crown.

Half a world away in South Asia, this iconography finds its echo in two ancient religions. Buddhism and Hinduism delve deep to uncover the link between chakras (the powerful energy centres that we carry inside of us) and the auras we radiate to the world.

In the 1800s, these ancient beliefs inspired a fresh generation of truth-seekers in the United States. Led by formidable psychic Helena Blavatsky, they called themselves the theosophists and dedicated themselves to exploring the deeper spiritual realities of life.

Can all this be a coincidence – a single vision shared by people from all corners of the globe, no matter the distance that divides them? The following pages explore how various cultures and peoples have envisioned the aura over the years and attempted to capture the phenomenon in words. The backdrop for their theories may change, along with the language they're written in, but surely so many generations of thinkers can't be wrong. The power of the aura is real!

✦ FIRST RECORDS ✦

Who drew the first pictorial aura? And where? Maybe someday we'll find the answer, scrawled in a cave or carved into the wall of an ancient tomb. Or maybe it'll always remain a mystery.

Thankfully, as far as written records go, we have more concrete evidence. Scholars are certain they've pinpointed the first written references to auras in a handful of ancient Hindi texts. Here, they're described as "prana" or "subtle breaths" – flowing through the bodies of each living thing, and out into the world in a beautiful bubble of light and colour.

IT IS ONLY WITH THE
HEART THAT ONE CAN SEE
RIGHTLY; WHAT IS ESSENTIAL
IS INVISIBLE TO THE EYE.

ANTOINE DE **SAINT-EXUPÉRY**

✦ BUILDING THE SUBTLE BODY ✦

Forget what you've heard about your eyes being windows to your soul. Your eyes will never give away quite as much as your aura.

There's no way you can shut down your aura or dim its light. It's like an unstoppable live transmission, beaming straight from your core in three technicolour dimensions. The question is, how? What is it about your aura that means it stays so in sync with your emotions?

To fathom this mystical connection, let's turn to Hinduism and Buddhism. Although two very distinct religions, both envision the aura as one part of a larger energy system called the "subtle body". Like an iceberg floating in uncharted waters, the roots of the subtle body extend deep beneath the skin. You'll never see the powerful energy centres at its core. The most you can ever hope to glimpse is the tip: the aura's outer glow.

The rest – seven chakras running down the length of the spine – stay hidden. Chakras are what give our auras *life*. While auras depict the state of energy around your body, chakras are all about channelling that energy, allowing it to flow through and from your body in a harmonious stream. It's no coincidence there are as many auric layers as there are chakras. Each chakra is connected to a particular auric layer, flooding it with colour and energy, and acting as a volume control for the frequency of its vibes.

When they're perfectly balanced, your aura will be singing with health, reaching into the world, making you feel that no dream is beyond your grasp. Conversely, blocked or out-of-balance chakras can leave you feeling overburdened, overwhelmed and ready to retreat into your shell.

✦ THE SEVEN CHAKRAS ✦

Nothing has more influence over the size, vibrancy and health of your aura than the chakras listed here.

CROWN CHAKRA, AKA *SAHASRARA*

Location: Atop your head.

Colour: Shades of violet, hinting at strong spiritual overtones.

Meaning: *Sahasrara* translates as "thousand-petalled lotus" and it couldn't be a better fit for this chakra, which is strongly connected to thought, wisdom and enlightenment. Open this regal chakra and you're sure to connect with your higher self. Signs of a balanced crown chakra are: a blissed-out, non-judgemental outlook and a deep sense of peace with yourself and the universe. Nagging ailments are alien to you. But once this chakra becomes blocked, you'll find your attention span start to wane and your physical issues return. Don't expect to smash your personal best or write your thesis until you've restored the balance.

Connects to: The causal body or ketheric template. This seventh, outermost layer of your aura offers an intriguing window into your past lives.

THIRD-EYE CHAKRA, AKA *AJNA*

Location: Between your eyebrows, just above the bridge of your nose.

Colour: Purple and indigo.

Meaning: It's no coincidence the third-eye chakra is close to the pineal gland – a mysterious, pine-cone-shaped part of the brain that's linked with perception, sleep cycles and light sensitivity. The third-eye chakra is all about vision and intuition. Opening it up can be a great way to push the limits of your five senses beyond what you'd normally perceive, allowing you to fine-tune your psychic abilities and open your mind to the world of auric energy. This synergy with the universe is a beautiful thing to experience; knowing you can rely on your intuition takes the angst out of decision-making. Symptoms of a blocked or closed third eye include endless deliberation, poor decision-making and trouble sleeping.

Connects to: The celestial body. If you're looking to tap into your subconscious or dip your toe into the spirit realm, this sixth auric layer can be your gateway.

THROAT CHAKRA, AKA *VISHUDDA*

Location: The centre of your throat.

Colour: Bright blue.

Meaning: This chakra is key to self-expression in all its forms – via singing, conversation, body language or even the written word. Open the throat chakra and you're guaranteed to find your voice, literally or metaphorically. Whatever you choose to read into that, a harmonious throat chakra can only be a blessing. *Vishudda* translates as "especially pure", and the experience of having your thoughts, needs or creative vision captured in words so perfectly can bring you endless joy and fulfilment. Whether you've been struggling for inspiration or putting off a tricky conversation with your significant other, a balanced throat chakra can be hugely useful in setting yourself up for success. Be sure to steer clear of junk food and polluted city streets as either one can block the throat chakra, leaving you feeling tongue-tied and overwhelmed with social anxiety.

Connects to: The etheric template. No wonder this fifth layer in your aura is all about speaking your truth – letting the whole world know what's in your soul.

HEART CHAKRA, AKA *ANAHATA*

Location: The centre of your chest. A little to the right of your physical heart.

Colour: Green (turning soft pink any time the energy frequency rises a little higher).

Meaning: Love, compassion, forgiveness. All these qualities – which colour our lives with meaning – begin and end with the heart chakra, an energy centre that's brimming with empathy and emotion. Without it, we'd be incapable of love or forgiveness, even for ourselves. So long as it stays balanced and open, you'll be blessed with a full heart – as well as the ability to forgive and forget. Just beware, if you find yourself becoming increasingly cold-hearted or cynical – keen to pick every fault you can find with yourself and others – a blocked heart chakra might just be to blame.

Connects to: The astral body. This all-important fourth layer of your aura is also known as the "bridge layer", because it connects your soul to the wider spirit realm.

SOLAR PLEXUS CHAKRA, AKA *MANIPURA*

Location: Midway between your heart and your belly button.

Colour: Vibrant yellow or shimmery gold – this chakra burns with all the energy and vitality of the sun.

Meaning: Call it what you will – the fire in your belly, your inner spark – this golden chakra is all about coming into your power and owning it. Its Sanskrit name – a conflation of the words for "city" and "gem" – paints a picture of treasures untold, which is exactly what an open solar plexus can bring. You'll feel competent, capable and blessed with the Midas touch, as if there's no limit to what you can achieve. Setting healthy boundaries to protect your energy will also come as second nature. A blocked solar plexus, however, could be the root of endless troubles, nixing your chances of attaining any personal goal.

Connects to: The mental body – the outermost of the three inner layers of your aura. These layers have a particularly strong connection to your physical body.

SACRAL CHAKRA, AKA *SVADHISTHANA*

Location: A few inches below your belly button.

Colour: A passionate and spicy shade of orange. The energy of this chakra is hot, hot, hot.

Meaning: Desire, sexuality and creativity (whether the result is an arty project or a brand-new life) all spring from the sacral chakra. Open up your sacral chakra and prepare to lose yourself in a world of sensation, emotion and sensuality. Small wonder its Sanskrit name – *Svadhisthana* – translates as "one's own place". In fact, the sacral chakra allows you to experience everyday life on a whole new level of emotional intensity. You'll also feel inspired to express yourself and be taken by a creative muse. If you're suffering from a lack of confidence or a low libido, you may want to spend some time rebalancing this chakra. A blocked sacral chakra could be the root of all your woes.

Connects to: The emotional body, the second, most vibrant layer of your aura.

ROOT CHAKRA, AKA *MULADHARA*

Location: The first and lowest of all the primary chakras, it sits at the very base of the spine.

Colour: Muted tones of red, brown and black.

Meaning: This earthbound chakra is all about laying strong foundations, for both auric health and life. Just as a tree puts down a system of roots to anchor itself, a balanced root chakra is essential for anyone wishing to feel properly grounded, connected with the natural world and safe in every sense. This chakra is strongly associated with home and family ties. Should your root chakra ever become blocked, you'll certainly know about it. A compromised root chakra can affect the stability of each chakra and auric layer in your energy system.

Connects to: The etheric body, the layer of your aura that manifests closest to your body.

YOU HAVE NO NEED
TO TRAVEL ANYWHERE.
JOURNEY WITHIN
YOURSELF, ENTER A MINE
OF RUBIES AND BATHE
IN THE SPLENDOUR OF
YOUR OWN LIGHT.

RUMI

✦ A WESTERN ODYSSEY ✦

For centuries, the subtle body has been the beating heart of Hinduism, Buddhism, yoga and Ayurvedic medicine. It took the Western world a little longer to catch on – with a helping hand from the trailblazing thinkers named below.

LIFE FORCE

Name: Baron Carl Ludwig von Reichenbach

Born: 1788, Stuttgart, Germany

Research obsession: Odic force

Need to know: Baron von Reichenbach started out as a gifted young chemist, until his wife's death sent him spiralling off track. He quit the city in favour of Reisenberg Castle, a lonely old pile out in the deep, dark woods.

Here he concocted the theory of "Odic force", the vital energy which he believed to emanate from every living thing. The name was inspired by Odin, fearsome ruler of the Norse gods, since the Baron was convinced he was dealing with an unstoppable force of nature made of the same stuff as the static that crackles in a darkening cloud.

When he wasn't out pacing the forest, the Baron would be testing his theories in darkened rooms with highly sensitive individuals. These subjects managed to see what the Baron never could – coloured lights glowing round magnets, crystals and even human hands.

LIGHTS IN THE DARK

Name: Walter John Kilner

Born: 1847, Suffolk, England

Research obsession: The "human atmosphere"

Need to know: During his endless shifts at St Thomas' Hospital, London, Kilner began seeing hints of mysterious energy around his patients' bodies. They'd even fluctuate throughout the patient's recovery. Intrigued, he devised a technique to bring these auras into focus. Peering through murky glass slides smeared with coal-tar dye (outlawed in the US for its "paranormal" properties), he spotted three layers in each aura.

PREACHING THE GOSPEL

Name: Charles Webster Leadbeater

Born: 1854, Stockport, England

Research obsession: All things theosophical

Need to know: Leadbeater was determined to push the doors of perception wide open, exposing the hidden astral plane beyond. A priest, teacher and truth seeker, Leadbeater was the silver-haired godfather of the theosophy movement. His obsession with the ancient beliefs of Buddhism and Hinduism led him halfway across the globe to Burma (now Myanmar) and Ceylon (modern-day Sri Lanka), where he immersed himself in the study of the subtle body under revered Indian masters. When he returned to England, he made it his mission to share his findings with Victorian society.

SPARKS OF INSPIRATION: KIRLIAN PHOTOGRAPHY

Fast-forward to 1935 and a rundown hospital in the Soviet Union, where level-headed engineer Semyon Kirlian discovered a whole new photography form – by accident.

Kirlian watched a patient being dosed with electricity while his hand rested on a photographic plate. When the man removed his hand, he left behind an image, burned onto the plate in ghostly tones. Kirlian could even make out a flash of electricity around the patient's skin.

Convinced he'd captured an actual aura on film, this day marked the beginning of a lifelong obsession for Kirlian. Sceptics may sniff at the credibility of his spiritual photography, but science is yet to fully explain the beautiful flares of colour in a more "rational" way.

✦ **GOOD VIBES ONLY** ✦

Auras are no longer the best-kept secret in South Asian medicine – or even underground knowledge whispered between a closed circle of theosophists.

Thanks to the rise of flower power in the 1960s – the era that gave us the Beach Boys' "Good Vibrations" (inspired by a dog that barked at anyone giving bad "cosmic energy") – vibes are so ingrained in today's culture, that references to their magic properties now seem commonplace.

How many times have you read, "no bad vibes" or "good vibes only", while scrolling through your Insta feed? Even if you haven't, the idea makes perfect emotional sense. We all understand instinctively how "vibes" work and the impact the energies of others can have on our own.

Our auras, after all, are hard-wired to seek out and draw in kindred spirits, others vibing at similar frequencies to us. You know that thrilling electric flutter you get when you're talking to someone and the two of you just effortlessly click? That's the magic of two auras aligning against all odds!

QUICK DEFINITION: VIBES/VIBRATIONS

Vibes (or vibrations) are waves of electromagnetic energy – and the stuff auras are made of. Their frequencies are set deep within your soul, inside the powerful energy centres that make you *you*.

They radiate out into the world, like Wi-Fi pulsing from a cosmic hotspot, in rainbow waves of energy. The space that these vibes take up – from your skin to the end of their reach – represents your personal energy field, aka your aura.

The frequency of these vibes can fluctuate from one moment to the next, depending on how you're feeling. And some layers of your aura are sure to be vibing at different frequencies than others (as a rule, the closer you move to the physical body, the lower the frequency). It's all part of the intricate spiritual signal you broadcast to the world, letting everyone in a two- to three-foot radius (the average reach of a human aura) know exactly what you're about without the need for words.

✦ OWN YOUR ENERGY, ✦ OWN YOUR POWER

When first impressions strike, lightning-fast and just as intense, they can be hard to negate. In moments when the pressure's on to show up as your most charismatic self, your aura can be your best friend. More than your clothes, your body language or even your words, it can communicate everything about your beliefs and qualities in an instant.

To be in control of your aura – knowing you can nurture and cleanse it of everything that's holding you back – is to be in control of the image you project to the world. If you're hoping to meet new friends, ditch the needy vibes and set your aura to: "I am the best company. I am adored." Or, to earn your co-workers' respect, try: "I am valued. I am capable of anything."

There's no more powerful way to magnetize the people and opportunities you desire than putting out similar vibes. Whatever you manifest in your energy is sure to come back to you tenfold.

✦ PROTECT YOUR ENERGY ✦

It's a superpower of your aura to call out to like-minded souls. But the further you reach with your energy, the more you'll realize nowhere is safe from bad vibes. Your aura is not just an energy field, it's a boundary, made to shield you from other energies. Mostly, it'll bounce away anything undesirable, but no aura is without its weak spots. Your emotional scars can sometimes manifest as literal holes in your aura, leaving you feeling vulnerable and triggered whenever bad vibes strike.

And that's not all. Sooner or later, you're bound to let someone into your life only to realize their energy is all wrong for you. At times like this, you'll need to set a boundary. And fast. No good ever came of mixing with "energy vampires" - toxic people who drain your energy and dim your light (we'll learn more about this on page 98). Get to know these auric red flags and you'll have the power to rid yourself of their harmful energies well before they outstay their welcome.

BIG BENEFITS FROM ONE LITTLE BOOK

You just reached the end of the first chapter. By now, you know plenty about auras in theory. Before we embark on the next phase of your journey, here's a reminder of the many life skills that will soon be yours.

★ If you're wondering about your well-being, a swift scan of your aura will act as a litmus test for the soul.

★ As a confident navigator of your auric layers, you'll be able to pinpoint exactly where your energies have become trapped or blocked – zones you need to cleanse and heal to let your colours shine.

★ Daily check-ins can help you protect your energy from toxic vibes. Becoming more attuned to others' energies is the best way to find your people, and to be a more compassionate friend.

★ The beam of light you radiate to the world will be yours to shape and control any way you choose, allowing you to magnetize the same energies back into your life.

NOTHING CAN DIM
THE LIGHT WHICH
SHINES FROM WITHIN.

MAYA ANGELOU

HOW TO
READ AURAS

In this chapter we'll attempt to connect you to your aura for the first time. We'll look at the myriad ways you can experience auras, offering tips to maximize your psychic potential. As well as discussing the matters of colour, shape and size and how to decode their subtle shades of meaning, we'll also delve deeper into the significance of each layer of your aura. But it's important to realize that, just as every aura in the world is unique, so is every person who connects with them. There's no way to predict how you will experience their dancing frequencies and shimmery colours. Excited? You should be!

✦ EXPERIENCING AURAS ✦

There's no two ways about it, the human aura is a startlingly beautiful phenomenon – a shimmering shell of light and energy, shifting all around us. Who wouldn't want a glimpse of that?

However much you're yearning for a first look into your soul, remember, not everyone is lucky enough to get a visual read on their aura from the get-go. You mustn't be too disheartened if you're not one of the lucky few who succeed immediately.

As with any new skill, it can take more than a little persistence and daily practice to manage to refocus your gaze, which is very likely set to filter out precisely the kind of hazy, peripheral visions we'll be looking to zero in on. That's a whole lifetime's worth of conditioning you have working against you. Even so, the great news is it's entirely possible to retrain your eye. Just because you can't see auras immediately doesn't mean you never will.

Even if you can make out something rather than nothing, your aura is unlikely to manifest in exactly the way you imagine. Some people see auric colours as a faint haze, clinging close to the skin, while others see splashes of colour on the physical body. The first rule of sensing auras is that there is no standard experience to be had from the techniques we're about to experiment with.

Indeed, much of what you intuit about spiritual energy fields – be it your own or another person's – may not even be seen at all...

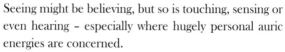

✦ EXTRASENSORY INTUITIONS ✦

Seeing might be believing, but so is touching, sensing or even hearing – especially where hugely personal auric energies are concerned.

At times, you might "sense" a colour or "feel" its influence, even if you're not getting the visual to match. A moment of contact, like a handshake, could be the thing to trigger these flashes of perception. Or perhaps it'll be a sound, echoing round another person, something that can only be a manifestation of their aura.

When these intuitions strike, it's important to honour them in the way they deserve – to lean into what they're telling you about your innate psychic abilities.

In books and movies, extrasensory perception (ESP) is often portrayed as a mystic ability – giving insight into events that ought to be beyond us – that you either have or you don't.

But the truth is far less black and white. Your "sixth sense" can show up in many surprising ways, since we are all born with more extrasensory abilities than you might think.

✦ MEET THE FIVE CLAIRS ✦

Read on to discover how you may have been sensing auras all along.

CLAIRVOYANCE – CLEAR SEEING
If you're blessed with clairvoyance, that makes you one of the lucky few for whom seeing auras comes naturally. Maybe you see with your actual eyes or maybe you're gazing through your mind's eye.

CLAIRAUDIENCE – CLEAR HEARING
If you've ever heard different frequencies around different people – like tuning into someone's own personal radio broadcast – then perhaps you're clairaudient.

CLAIRSENTIENCE – CLEAR FEELING
If you're a sponge for the emotions of others, and you're often walking into rooms and feeling overwhelmed by the vibes, then you might just be clairsentient.

CLAIRTANGENCY – CLEAR TOUCHING
Ever reached out to shake a person's hand and gained a flash of insight into the energy that surrounds them? If so, clairtangency could be one of your many talents.

CLAIRCOGNIZANCE – CLEAR KNOWING

Do your friends love you for your knack of grasping their emotional state, without the need for words? If you're blessed with this uncanny knowledge, then perhaps claircognizance is your superpower.

✦ EXPLORING YOUR AURA: FIRST STEPS ✦

Did you recognize yourself among the line-up of clairs? Now that you know a little more about how you experience auric energy, there's no better time to get hands-on with your aura by trying some of these simple exercises.

Maybe you'll feel drawn to one exercise in particular – one that speaks to your unique way of sensing auric energy. Trust in these whispers of intuition and know it's the very best way to cultivate and amplify your innate gifts.

Equally, please don't give up on other exercises that don't immediately inspire you. To really get the most out of them, you'll need to practise every day. Build them into your routine for a few days straight and you may soon start to see results.

✦ YOUR SACRED SPACE ✦

Before you get started, take a moment to consider when and where you'll be practising. Above all, your chosen space needs to be:

- ★ Peaceful – free from distractions and noise.
- ★ Perfectly lit – soft lighting should complement your visions, not drown them out.
- ★ Cozy and comfortable – to put you in the perfect mindset to welcome spiritual energies and sensations in.
- ★ Somewhere you can access whenever you want to tune in to your abilities.

Your favourite reading nook or your bed – a peaceful sanctuary where you feel safe – is an ideal choice. Inviting spiritual energies in on a daily basis will only strengthen your connection to these spaces.

Timing your practices consistently is another way to get the most out of them. You could try first thing in the morning, when you're in need of an energy boost, or last thing at night, when you're feeling relaxed and ready to drift into a dreamlike state.

✦ EXERCISE: A BALL OF ENERGY ✦

Calling all clairtangents! If you were born with the touch, then this exercise is tailor-made for you. With practice, this exercise will let you feel the energy of your aura, pulsing between your hands in a concentrated ball.

★ Ensure you're sitting comfortably as this will keep you feeling strong and grounded.

★ Take a few minutes to focus on your breath, allowing your mind to empty of any nagging thoughts.

★ Rub your hands together, like you just came in from the cold, for around 15 seconds, keeping your attention on your breath as you do so.

★ Still your hands and clasp them together. Now take a long, deep breath in and out.

★ Slowly begin to inch your hands apart. If it feels right, you can close your eyes at this point. When your hands are about a third of a metre apart, you can stop – hold for a few breaths.

★ At the same slow pace, move your hands back together. Focus on when the energy between your hands becomes so compact it's like you're holding something tangible. This is the right time to pause your hands.

★ What you have right now, between your hands, is the very essence of your aura – all seven layers – packed into a tight little ball of energy.

HOW TO USE YOUR AURA

★ Take the pure life-force energy in your hands and apply it to any part of your physical body or your aura that's in need of a little extra TLC. This is similar to laying healing hands on your skin.

★ If you're in need of a quick pick-me-up, try sweeping your hands across your face to refresh and energize you for the day.

REFINING THE BALL OF ENERGY

If this exercise left you empty-handed, please don't overthink it, or angst over the reasons why. It can take a few goes to overcome your ego – the sceptical voice inside your head that tells you, "This can't work" – and let your intuitions flow.

Next time, try repeating the exercise with a tiny adjustment. If you kept your eyes open, try closing them to focus your attention inward. If you had your eyes shut, do the opposite.

Try repeating affirmations – some positive statements – before you begin, to help build your belief in the power of your intuition. You could even try speaking directly to your physical body, asking it to let you access the energies between your hands.

The faintest tingle in your palms, or a hint of warmth, may be a sign you're on the right track.

✦ AMPING UP YOUR INTUITION ✦

Remember the third-eye chakra, the powerful energy centre between your eyes? This chakra is queen of intuition, which is a must for anyone looking to fine-tune their psychic abilities.

EXERCISE: MAGIC MEDITATIONS

Schedule in a daily meditation and you should see a difference in the quality of the intuitions that come your way. Here's an easy meditation to get you started:

⭑ Bring your attention to your breath, allowing thoughts to drift freely through your mind. You can notice their presence, like clouds on the horizon, without engaging with them.

⭑ Chant "om" (pronounced "aum") throughout. All chakras are responsive to sound and this particular mantra is the key you need to unlock the potential of your third eye.

⭑ Focus your mind's eye on the all-important space between your brows – and the magic that's surely happening here.

EXERCISE: NEVER UNDERESTIMATE THE POWER OF PURPLE

The visual equivalent of "om" is the colour purple, which can serve as another trigger to harness the magic of your third eye.

★ Start with a few deep, calming breaths.

★ Picture a shimmering ball of purple energy between your brows, glowing with health.

★ With every inhale, imagine the energy becoming bigger and brighter, until your whole body is immersed in its beautiful radiance.

EXERCISE: CRYSTAL VISIONS

This ritual calls for a gemstone. Amethyst, tanzanite, purple fluorite and labradorite all make perfect choices. As long as it's purple (the signature shade of the third-eye chakra), you're onto a winner.

★ Lie down and place your gemstone on your third eye and let it rest for 20 minutes.

★ Afterwards, carry your crystal with you everywhere, as a reminder of the energy you just invited into your world.

EXERCISE: INTUITIVE COLOURING

Mindful colouring can be a fun way to unwind. But what if there were more to it? Let your creative energies flow, and you'll be surprised at what else you set in motion.

- ⭐ Spend a few moments breathing, until your mind feels still.

- ⭐ Grab your coloured pens or pencils. Spread them in front of you in an inspiring fan.

- ⭐ Call on your intuition to guide you to the shades you need.

- ⭐ Without thinking, reach out to the colours and surrender to your instincts, however subtle.

- ⭐ Put pen to paper and colour to your heart's content. Only stop when the picture feels complete – a perfect snapshot of your auric colours in this moment.

THE EYES HAVE IT:
A NEW WAY OF SEEING

Now we've nurtured your third eye, it's time to consider your physical eyes. Your everyday vision may seem crystal-clear, but it's also heavily filtered by the ever-rational ego. Adjusting your gaze to see hazy spiritual energies doesn't always come easy. But once you get the knack of switching focus, it'll feel a little more natural every time you try. Especially with these handy beginner's tips.

★ Experiment with different ways of "looking". Relax your eyes, so everything slips out of focus. Or try observing your subject out of the corner of your eye rather than head-on. Explore your peripheral vision, a mysterious space where "reality" begins to blur, and you'll be amazed at what you see.

★ Go easy on your eyes as relearning how to see is bound to put a strain on them. Try not to practise for longer than a few minutes and never when you're tired.

★ If you wear glasses or contact lenses, try scanning for auras with and without them. The results may surprise you.

EXERCISE: SHADOW AURAS

You've felt your auric energy. But there's nothing like seeing it with your eyes. Here's how you can develop this skill.

* Settle down in front of a neutral wall. If your wall's painted a distinct colour, a sheet of paper can help provide the blank canvas you need.

* Take a few calming breaths and rub your hands to spark your energy.

* Let your gaze land on whichever finger you feel drawn to (often your ring finger).

* Focus on the tip, then slowly let your gaze slip away to the left. Once your other fingers become blurry points in your peripheral vision, stop. This is the perspective to hold.

* Breathe and relax. Any moment now, your auric energy may reveal itself, in the shape of a shimmery grey shadow, radiating from your fingers. What you're seeing is very likely the first layer of your aura (the one that clings closest to your body): the etheric body.

EXERCISE: A SELF-PORTRAIT

You've seen shadows and sparks, but now you probably want the full-colour, 3-D experience. By building on everything you've learned so far, this exercise lets you see yourself like never before: your whole body, surrounded by layer-upon-layer of rainbow-coloured vibes.

★ Stand or sit in front of a full-length mirror.

★ Rub your hands until you feel the energy dancing between your palms. Close your eyes, take a breath and turn your palms up to the sky. Place them on your lap in a gesture that says you are open to whatever the universe has to offer. Now, take a few grounding breaths, and enjoy being fully in this moment.

★ Open your eyes and look directly at your reflection. Then, let your gaze slide slowly off to the left. When your reflected eyes are in your peripheral vision, you'll know you've found the sweet spot. Hold your focus and breathe through it. Any moment now, you'll see your etheric body manifest as a flickering halo over to the left.

★ This is a sign it's time to expand your focus. Do this subtly, one inhale at a time. With each breath you take, move your body back from the glass by a fraction. After each tiny movement, pause to take in your new perspective. Pay attention to your senses, sensations and breath as you immerse yourself in the full experience of your aura.

★ If your focus is broken and you lose sight of the etheric body, don't push yourself to try again. It takes time and patience to discover how best to connect with your own energy field. Just know that everything is unfolding exactly as it should, and your colours will reveal themselves at the perfect moment for you.

✦ READING ANOTHER PERSON'S AURA ✦

Now you've glimpsed your own energy, reading the auras of others – friends and family, pets and plants – is a natural next step. The techniques we've explored are all adaptable to others, especially the exercise on page 54, which won't even require a mirror this time around. All you'll really need is a supportive friend with an open mind and a blank white wall for them to stand in front of.

Reading the energies of others can be more straightforward than reading your own. Even on a good day, it's hard to look at yourself through eyes that are completely unclouded by self-judgement or preconceptions.

Scanning someone else's aura can be a way to put your intuition to the test. You can even practise on strangers while you're out and about, from the person next to you in line to someone you rubbed shoulders with at a gig. As your intuition strengthens, you'll find you can do so, even without a blank backdrop to make the colours pop. There's nothing like a concert to make your heart beat faster and your vibes shine brighter. Tuning into the energies of the crowd can be an exhilarating experience.

Just be mindful of the nature of the vibes you're connecting with before you feel fully in control of your own boundaries (more on this later). It can be oh-so easy to absorb the negative energies of others.

If in doubt, let your intuition guide you. If the energy you're reading leaves you feeling warm and fuzzy, you're on to a good thing. But if something feels off, it could well be time to take a step back. Those warning prickles, the sudden tension in your body, is your intuition trying to tell you something important. And it never lies.

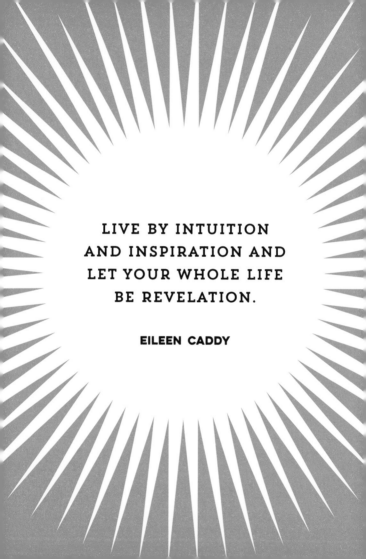

LIVE BY INTUITION
AND INSPIRATION AND
LET YOUR WHOLE LIFE
BE REVELATION.

EILEEN CADDY

✦ SHADES OF MEANING ✦

As intuition takes hold, deepening your skills as an aura reader, you'll notice more and more shades orbiting in your auric field. Each new colour has its own unique meaning: a message about some aspect of your soul, mind or body that's just waiting to be decoded. And as you read on, you'll learn how.

In the following pages we'll discuss the most common auric colours and start to interpret their ever-changing shades. It's more of a subtle art than an exact science, depending on the layer each colour manifests in and, crucially, its vibrancy.

When your colours are deep, rich and dancing with intensity, you can interpret them in their purest sense. On days when your colours appear lacklustre, muddied and drained of all vibrancy, the meaning too becomes clouded, a sure sign your soul is in need of a little rest and relaxation.

✦ RED ✦

Does your aura burn with fiery shades? If so, you must have your feet firmly on the ground, with a realistic outlook on life (remember red's link with the root chakra?). A bright red shade signals health, vitality and strength of character. You're also likely a very physical being, who revels in exercise, touch, fine dining and the great outdoors – all of which are like a balm to your soul. You're also prone to seeing red figuratively, so be mindful of that short fuse of yours.

DULL AND LACKLUSTRE

If your powerful red turns muddy, it may be time to find a healthier outlet for your anger, before you become trapped in a spiral of sleepless nights and obsessive thinking. Exercise and meditation may help you reclaim a little peace of mind. But if you're still struggling to let go, you can also try the energy cleanse on page 118. There's no better way to banish troublesome negative energies from your aura.

✦ ORANGE ✦

If your energy is dancing with orange vibes, then others are sure to seek you out and follow your lead. Your zesty energy is seriously infectious. A free spirit with a lust for life, you can't resist the thrill of a new adventure. You don't care about the destination, so long as the journey is joyful. And that's something you'll always make sure of.

You're every bit as in tune with your body as a "red" personality. But don't get too hung up on appearances and shallow connections. Spend some time connecting with people on a deeper level and you're sure to find the right balance.

DULL AND LACKLUSTRE

When orange vibes give way to brown, you may feel you've lost your creative spark and become mired in your own bad habits. Have you become addicted to doomscrolling on social media? Or something even more damaging? If so, consider this a spiritual red flag, letting you know it's time to make a change. See page 94 for tips on having a digital detox.

✦ YELLOW ✦

If yellow is your vibe, then let it shine! Like a literal ray of sunshine, you bring laughter and light into the lives of everyone around you. Your family and friends adore you for your open mind and your happy-go-lucky approach to life. In their eyes, you'll always be a beacon of hope, inspiration and creativity.

You can also be pretty determined when you set your mind to something. Learning is your lifelong passion and you are often found with your head in a book – or immersed in some other kind of study.

DULL AND LACKLUSTRE

All work and no play is a sure-fire way to dim your yellow light. Now's the time to step away from your latest project and get back to your loved ones.

✦ GREEN ✦

All the best connotations of this earthbound colour – growth, nurturing, healing – are yours and more. A genuine earth mother (or father) to everyone around you, your huge, open heart is the source of your strength, and your ability to lavish love and kindness on others your unique superpower. You're rarely lacking in anything thanks to your faith in the universe – and a deep-seated belief that it will always provide for you. Chances are you already have a successful career in a highly caring profession. Just don't lose sight of your own needs in your selfless quest to fix everyone you meet.

DULL AND LACKLUSTRE

If your leafy green is starting to wither on the vine, it may be time to take a long hard look at where you're focusing your energies. Alas, greens are all too prone to jealousy. Try to focus on the abundance of blessings in your own life instead.

✦ BLUE ✦

It's no coincidence that blue is the colour of the throat chakra, making self-expression your greatest gift. You're a natural communicator, so it's no wonder you inspire such passion and confidence in everyone who hears you speak. By now, you must be aware of the power of your words, and keen to use it for the greater good. Don't fight these higher instincts, they're guaranteed to steer you in the right direction.

You're a highly creative individual, who possesses imagination and flair in spades. Make time for all the pursuits that nourish your soul – whether that's painting, writing, teaching or mentoring others – and you won't regret it.

DULL AND LACKLUSTRE

You know why they call it "the blues", right? Because the flipside of this colour is low energy and low mood. When you see your colour start to dim, it's important to ask a few tough questions of yourself. At work, for instance, are you guiding your team or controlling them?

✦ TURQUOISE ✦

It's not every day you glimpse a turquoise aura. Conjuring images of tropical seas and precious stones, this colour goes hand in hand with a blissfully balanced state of mind – and a particular kind of hard-won wisdom. Turquoise individuals are typically old souls, with a deep connection to the spirit realm. The impulse to give back and nurture others is strong, as well as uncovering and reviving the long-lost wisdom of our ancestors. Turquoises are often found in teaching and coaching jobs, shining their light into the world.

DULL AND LACKLUSTRE

This special shade is rarely anything less than vibrant – positively dancing with vitality and inspiration. In the unlikely event that your magic starts to fade, you should endeavour to keep out of others' business and focus your energies on the work that makes you shine brightest.

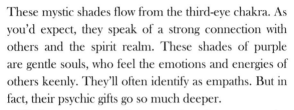

✦ PURPLE, INDIGO AND VIOLET ✦

These mystic shades flow from the third-eye chakra. As you'd expect, they speak of a strong connection with others and the spirit realm. These shades of purple are gentle souls, who feel the emotions and energies of others keenly. They'll often identify as empaths. But in fact, their psychic gifts go so much deeper.

Kindness comes easily to purples; they possess the knack of making everyone around them feel seen and understood. One wave of their all-embracing energy is all it takes. Your favourite teacher at school, that speaker who made you believe you could – they're very likely nurturing purples too.

DULL AND LACKLUSTRE

Purples spend their days swimming in a sea of energies and emotions, none of which belong to them. Let the wrong ones in, and you're sure to go from being a sensitive violet to a shrinking one. When this happens, your only option is to cleanse and protect your own precious colours.

✦ CRYSTAL ✦

Even in a sea of colours, there's one dreamy, opalescent aura that will always stand out – the crystal aura. If this happens to be your flow, then that makes you rare, beautiful and born with your own kind of magic.

The ultimate empaths, crystals have a chameleon-like ability to absorb the mood of whoever comes near them, then reflect it back like a mirror. If you're crystal, your compassion is your superpower, enabling you to heal the most damaged individuals. But it can also be your kryptonite.

Crystals struggle with setting boundaries to protect their energy. Relationships can prove tricky to navigate too. Who could ever hope to understand a crystal on the deep instinctual level that the crystal understands them?

DULL AND LACKLUSTRE

When compassion fatigue sets in, time outdoors, communing with the beautiful natural world, can be a powerful tonic for crystals. Such moments can leave you feeling recentred and revitalized.

✦ BLACK AND GREY ✦

Did your energy just turn dark and stormy? If so, don't panic; this isn't who you are. Perhaps you're feeling unwell, grieving or going through a particularly challenging moment.

Whatever the reason, black's a sign your aura is vibing at a lower frequency than usual. Black spots can indicate trapped energies in your aura, including unprocessed anger. But a shut-down aura is also a safe aura, protected from further triggers and bad vibes, so don't despair if you see patches of darker energy blocking your flow every now and again. As long as this doesn't become your new normal, it's no cause for concern.

Grey flecks tell a similar tale that your vibrant energies have been depleted.

DULL AND LACKLUSTRE

When glossy blacks turn murky, it's time to take a deeper look at your energy. Are you holding onto a grudge that's bringing you down? The hurt could be buried even deeper, in one of your past lives. A professional aura reader may be able to shed light on your intriguing backstory.

OTHER COLOURS YOU MAY GLIMPSE

★ White is not only the default colour of the etheric body. Indeed, you may also see white flashes in any other auric layer, symbolizing a pure heart and new beginnings. White energy can feel like a breath of fresh air, breezing into your life along with a world of possibilities. White can also act as a protective shield, keeping your precious energy safe.

★ When white intensifies, in beautiful shimmers of silver, it marks a special kind of awakening. Silver flecks in your aura are like a badge of honour, earned through meditation, acts of kindness and compassionate thoughts. Silver is also the hallmark of a gifted psychic, with a strong connection to the spirit realm – almost as if they've been touched by the divine.

★ Gold is another hallmark of an especially enlightened being, someone whose aura has been forever transformed by meditation and the acts of kindness they've lavished on others. Time spent this way is truly golden, bringing you heavenly spiritual protection.

✦ SEVEN MAGIC LAYERS ✦
OF MEANING

So far, we've put our intuition to the test and run through a primer of auric colours. Now it's time to add the final piece to the puzzle: the secret knowledge that will elevate your readings above and beyond. In short, it's not only a question of which colours you're seeing, but where.

To help you target your readings and your healing, we'll unveil all seven layers of the aura, revealing how each one speaks of your inner state. Starting with the low-energy etheric body, we'll radiate out from your body, growing in strength with each new layer, till we reach the outer limits of your auric field and the high-vibing causal plane.

Despite the power of this seventh outer layer, which broadcasts your vibe to the world, it's important to realize that the causal plane is nothing without a solid foundation beneath.

Your aura is a finely balanced ecosystem. If you want to ensure the health of the whole, you'll need to nourish every single layer in its make-up.

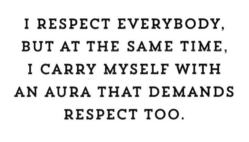

I RESPECT EVERYBODY,
BUT AT THE SAME TIME,
I CARRY MYSELF WITH
AN AURA THAT DEMANDS
RESPECT TOO.

LIL' KIM

LAYER 1: THE ETHERIC BODY

Typical colour: White or bluish grey.

Indicates: Physical and emotional health.

Position: Next to the physical body.

Essential facts: Have you ever spotted a silvery glow, clinging to your body like a second skin? If so, then perhaps you've already glimpsed the etheric body for yourself. No other auric layer is quite so visible to the naked eye. Pulsing at a lower frequency than the other layers, its close link with the root chakra means the etheric body has everything to do with your connection to mother earth and the physical body. If you're after a litmus test of your well-being, there's no better layer to focus on. Maybe you're feeling energized and ready to run a marathon. Or maybe you're laid up with the flu and contemplating a Netflix marathon. Either way, it's sure to be reflected in the etheric body.

For more active individuals, the energy contained in the etheric body packs a dazzling punch - it's the dynamo that drives them over the finish line. Conversely, if your routine is more sedentary (perhaps you work an office job), you'd expect this layer to be much less vibrant.

Heal this layer: Aside from rushing to the gym, there is another way to replenish this layer. Indulging in a few home comforts can work wonders. The root chakra is all about earthly pleasures and enjoying a comfortable home environment. Something as simple as a soak in the bath, or a hug from a loved one could be a great way to leave you feeling refreshed and recentred.

LAYER 2: THE EMOTIONAL BODY

Typical colour: Any shade of the rainbow.

Indicates: Your ever-changing emotions.

Position: Second layer from your physical body.

Essential facts: Linked with the sacral chakra, this layer paints an animated picture of your emotions in swirling clouds of colour. No other auric layer is painted with such beautiful, expressive shades. Though very much of the moment (like your mood), the emotional body also bears the taint of your memories. Certain experiences are bound to leave a stain, and nothing muddies the colours of this layer like stress. It's how you deal with it that counts. Perhaps you've been burying your feelings, or holding on when it's time to let go. If so, these emotions are sure to resurface with a vengeance as dark patches of negative energy, clogging up the emotional layer. On days when you feel edgy, argumentative and made of eggshell, it's worth doing some healing on your emotional layer.

This layer is also hugely responsive to its surroundings. From the moment you walk into a room, it can help you read the vibe and recognize your tribe. In certain circumstances – when making a speech or attending an interview, for instance – it might reach out and interact with the energies of others in the room: another superpower of the emotional body.

Heal this layer: Whenever you're feeling stuck – overwhelmed by negative thoughts or an argument that never ends – try heading out for a walk or opening a window. A breath of fresh air can work wonders for the energy levels in this layer. You could also try the energy cleanse on page 118. Connecting with trapped pockets of energy can be a crucial step in freeing yourself of their influence, leaving you more energy to devote to the people and things that bring you joy.

LAYER 3: THE MENTAL BODY

Typical colour: Shimmery yellow, sparking with the energy of the solar plexus chakra.

Indicates: Thoughts, values and personal belief systems.

Position: Third from the physical body; the last of the inner layers of the aura.

Essential facts: If you're looking to glimpse the mental body, it pays to focus on your head and shoulders. This is where your glow burns brightest, because this layer represents all things cerebral. Your thoughts, belief systems, everything you need to piece together your own version of reality is reflected in this layer. It's like the golden filter that colours your vision of the world.

It also speaks volumes about your self-image, as shaped by the ego. The ego (in Freudian terms) is the inner voice that speaks to us all, helping us rationalize the behaviour of others or talking us out of risky choices.

But does that make it a best friend or a sabotaging frenemy? A weak and depleted mental body, taking up a fraction of the space that it ought to occupy, can be a serious red flag, showing that you may need to dial back the self-deprecation and be kinder to yourself.

When you're in a more positive headspace, this layer swells and positively sings with health. If you happen to be a student or anyone with a passion for learning, you might even see this layer begin to spark with tiny flames of inspiration and enthusiasm. That's how you'll truly know you've hit your streak and come into your creative power.

Heal this layer: Deploy positive affirmations and empowering mantras about everything that you are and everything that you deserve. It's the first step on the long path to breaking a vicious cycle of negative beliefs.

LAYER 4: THE ASTRAL BODY

Typical colour: Rosy-pink, pulsing with the energy of the heart chakra.

Indicates: What's in your heart.

Position: If we were to draw a line between the inner auric layers (most closely tied to our earthly bodies) and the outer ones – linked to all the mysterious qualities that make us spiritual beings – this fourth layer would be it.

Essential facts: Its link with the heart chakra, an eternal spring of empathy, compassion and unconditional love, lends the astral layer a special kind of magic. Whether you're wanting to tap into the elusive spiritual realm or connect with a like-minded new friend (someone whose energy meshes so perfectly with your own), the astral body is the go-between that makes it happen. For this reason, it's often called the "bridge layer".

The astral body is also strongly linked with instinct and intuition. To "follow your heart" is to tap into the flow of this layer – whether you realize you're doing it or not.

When your astral body is in the pink, aglow with gratitude and love for everyone in your life (not least yourself), it can be a powerful, self-perpetuating force. Radiating this rosy image out into the world can't fail to attract new connections and opportunities.

When you're not living *la vie en rose*, the astral body can be harshly impacted. Its affinity for the energies of others makes it extremely susceptible to bad vibes, similar to those you'd experience in a break-up, so you'll need to guard this layer against heartbreak in all forms. Whether you're losing a lover or grieving a loss, taking care of your aura is a must (as explored later on).

Heal this layer: Nurturing self-talk can be healing. Next time you catch yourself taking a harsh tone, try to practise self-kindness and you'll reap the rewards.

LAYER 5: THE ETHERIC TEMPLATE

Typical colour: Varies, but ideally an ice-cool blue – to mirror the expressive energy of the throat chakra.

Indicates: Everything about who you are and the pulse of your own unique energy.

Position: Fifth from the body; this occupies a space between one and two feet wide.

Essential facts: If you're wondering about the purpose of the etheric template, then the clue's in the name. Positioned on the far side of the bridge layer, the etheric template is a deeply spiritual layer with strong ties to the physical realm. Contained within this layer, you'll find a blueprint for everything that you are, encompassing your physical form, your personality and the vibes that you broadcast to the world. Such is the synergy between this spiritual layer and your physical being that, if you're unlucky enough to fall ill, symptoms will manifest here in your auric field before you ever notice them in your body.

Thanks to its link with the throat chakra, this layer is hugely responsive to sound, music and song – all of which are sure-fire ways to unlock its creative and expressive power. For people who fully inhabit this layer, connecting with others is blissfully straightforward, thanks to the warm, expressive energy they radiate to the world.

Heal this layer: It's not always easy to speak your truth. But you'll know if you've been ignoring your inner voice too long, because it's sure to take the shine off your etheric template. If you find yourself becoming cynical and withdrawn, it's time to lift your energy by indulging in one of your favourite creative pursuits. Whether you paint, dance, write or scream your pent-up emotions out of your system, self-expression is the antidote you need to restore your vibes to a shimmering state of health.

LAYER 6: THE CELESTIAL BODY

Typical colour: There's nothing typical about this ethereal and notoriously hard to glimpse layer of your aura. When it appears, it can take on shifting pastel shades – with the same rainbow lustre as mother of pearl.

Indicates: This layer acts as a window into your subconscious mind and sings of the power of your intuition.

Position: Sixth from your body, with a reach of somewhere between two and three feet.

Essential facts: Ever wondered where your hopes and dreams are stored? The celestial body is the library of all your best fantasies – the soulmate you hope to cross paths with, that trip you long to take – and so much more. Contained in this magic layer, you'll find all the energy you need to manifest these dreams into reality.

Awash with the shimmering light of your intuition (which flows from your third-eye chakra), this layer can be your gateway to the spirit realm, allowing you to connect with your higher self and open your mind to messages from your spirit guides.

The essence of this layer is pure love and light – those who inhabit it fully are blessed with a readiness to forgive and forget, accepting themselves and others for exactly who they are. In fact, there's no surer path to inner peace and unconditional love.

Heal this layer: In your more pessimistic moments, when your dreams seem hopelessly out of reach, don't despair. There's a real alternative to sitting around, waiting for the situation to fix itself. Work on your celestial layer, nourishing it with daily mantras and meditations, and you'll soon start seeing things in a different (pearly pastel) light. With intuition whispering in your ear, you'll be perfectly placed to make your dreams come true.

LAYER 7: THE CAUSAL PLANE

Typical colour: On a good day, this layer shimmers with dazzling gold or pure white light.

Indicates: This striking spiritual template shows you your past and your future: everything you are and everything you could become.

Position: The outermost layer of your aura has a high vibration and an astonishing reach, spanning anywhere between three and five feet, depending on your mood and the stability of your lower layers.

Essential facts: Like a high-vibing super beam from within, the causal plane is powered by the mighty crown chakra. The end of its reach marks the end of your auric field. Beyond this point, there's only the cosmic plane. So consider this layer your own personal link with the divine – or whatever higher power you choose to believe in.

Its powerful energy encircles every other layer in your aura, providing much-needed balance and cohesion throughout the whole of your energy field.

One of its other names is the "ketheric template", hinting at the intriguing information that's stored within its flow. In fact, this layer contains a blueprint for the whole of your spiritual journey through life – even the parts you can't remember. As well as the experiences you've been marked by this time around, the causal layer is also coloured by significant events in your past lives. Even if these defining moments are lost from your memory, they'll always have a place in the causal plane, flowing through your energy field along with your other beautiful colours.

Heal this layer: Ever felt trapped in an impossible dilemma or an unhelpful spiral of thoughts that led you nowhere? Feeling stuck is a sure sign that all is not well with your causal layer. As for the remedy? It's as simple as working to unblock your crown chakra, with deep, reflective meditation.

✦ SEEING SHAPES ✦

At this point, you're learning to be a super-sensitive seer of auras as well as well-versed in the hidden meanings of colour, size and vibrancy. But did you know that shape matters too? Your aura won't always manifest as a textbook oval. At times, it could morph into the following shapes and patterns:

⭐ **Fuzzy:** Finding it hard to tell where your aura ends and the world begins? Forever getting caught up in other people's drama? Then you'd better put down some boundaries. And fast.

⭐ **The wall:** You'll never compromise on your boundaries. But behind your impenetrable energy block, it's sure to get lonely.

⭐ **Spiky:** When your energy turns prickly, it's a telltale sign you've been hurt before. Just be sure you're not pushing away the pure-hearted people who genuinely want to help you heal.

⭐ **Smooth/regular oval:** If your aura is neutral, then congratulations. Your healthy boundaries help you to enjoy interacting with the energies of others, while feeling happy in your own skin.

IF YOU HAVE TRUE
GRATITUDE, IT WILL
EXPRESS ITSELF
AUTOMATICALLY.
IT WILL BE VISIBLE
IN YOUR EYES, AROUND
YOUR BEING,
IN YOUR AURA.

SRI CHINMOY

AURAS IN
EVERYDAY LIFE

Your aura is the compass you need to plot your course through life. Harness its magic and there's no limit to the people and opportunities you can attract into your orbit.

This chapter is filled with the inspiration you need to make your aura work for you, with tips on how to date more mindfully (based on smouldering colour-based chemistry), turn your home into a haven of rejuvenating colours, smash your goals at work, and make mindful make-up and wardrobe choices that serve you every day.

We'll also consider your daily routine, looking at how you can build in time to cleanse and heal your way to perfect spiritual health.

✦ SELF-CARE FOR THE SOUL ✦

Whether you're the kind of person who can't leave the house until you've blow-dried your hair, or you swear by a three-step skincare regime that never fails to lift your mood, we all have our daily routines – rituals that leave us feeling lighter, brighter and ready to face the day ahead.

But here's the thing. Your aura is just as deserving of love and attention as your face or your hair. And if you can find even a few moments in your hectic day to schedule in some spiritual self-care, then you'll always be thankful you did.

You might not need a full-on energy cleanse, sweeping through all seven of your auric layers (more on this later), but you can never shine too brightly. If you keep your energy at its most magnetic, showing all you have to offer as a friend, employee or lover, there's no telling what – or who – you might attract into your life.

These helpful hacks will help you boost your energies and restore your sparkle in minutes.

TAKE AN ENERGY SHOWER

When bad vibes or unkind words strike, and you can't seem to let them go, this ritual will help you wash them all away. As you stand in the shower, beneath the soothing jets of water, picture your grievances – some unkind words or rude manners perhaps – as insignificant specks of dust, washing out of your hair and straight down the plughole, where they belong. Now turn your attention to the water. Visualize it flowing through all seven layers of your aura, before it touches your physical body. Feel its warm, soothing influence wash through your energy field, cleansing everywhere it touches.

TREAT YOURSELF TO SOME SWEET SELF-TALK

Want to give your aura the ultimate glow-up? Then it's time to get vocal and give some serious thought as to how you've been speaking to yourself.

If you're in the habit of putting yourself down, hating on your appearance, your competency, even your lovability, you may not notice the effect it has on you. But the truth is, these harsh words linger in your auric layers – clouding your astral and mental bodies – long after you think or utter them out loud.

To repair the damage, try to schedule in a daily meditation, based around loving mantras and affirmations. You can tailor your words in any way you choose. Just as long as you start with: "I am..." With these two little words, you can work untold magic. Speak them like an incantation to manifest your wishes in your consciousness, in your energy and out in the world. Here are some examples to get your inspiration flowing:

You desire: More friends.
Try: "I am uniquely me and the most caring, fun friend a person could hope to meet."

You desire: A promotion.
Try: "I am a perfect fit for this amazing new role. I am ready to achieve incredible things together with my new team."

You desire: An aura of quiet confidence.
Try: "I am more than enough."

You desire: A dream date.
Try: "I am beautiful, inside and out, and can't help but radiate this to the world. To know me is to love me."

You desire: To distance yourself from toxic personalities.
Try: "I am attractive only to those who will enrich my life with their positive vibes."

You desire: To let bygones be bygones.
Try: "I am ready to let go of all that no longer serves me."

SMILE... AND YOUR AURA SMILES WITH YOU

Nothing colours your aura quite like emotion. And so your smile can be your secret weapon – an instant pick-me-up that reinvigorates your colours in seconds. The next time you feel your energy start to wane, crack a smile. As you do so, imagine a rainbow of shades appearing above your head. Inhale deeply and with each breath imagine your smile spreading and the rainbow widening, as its beautiful colours begin to sparkle. Do you feel those warm, fuzzy endorphins flowing yet?

CONSIDER A DIGITAL DETOX

In today's society, it's perfectly normal for many of us to spend our days glued to a screen, whether it's a laptop at work or a smartphone at home. The pressure to stay in touch with your tribe and to present a picture-perfect version of yourself on social media is real. Those long hours spent doomscrolling, lurking on your crush's social media feed, or comparing your own life with the airbrushed perfection of the average influencer can't help but take a toll on your energy levels. If you start to feel a heaviness in your soul as you replay that reel for the umpteenth time, then it could be a sign to put down your device. Now's a great time to reconnect with your energy via a healing meditation or visualization.

If cutting back on screen time is not an option, then you may want to fill your home with lepidolite, a gemstone that can protect your energy from the technology that's draining it. Try placing crystals by your TV, your bed – anywhere that you know you'll be exposed. Its stunning purple shade makes it an attractive addition to any home.

A RECIPE FOR AURIC HEALTH

There's no way to separate your spiritual body from your physical body. The two stay absolutely intertwined, from the moment we're born till the moment we die. So it's no surprise your diet impacts your aura as much as it does your waistline. If you've been surviving on a menu of processed junk, you can't expect the colours of your aura to be aglow with health. Instead, they're likely to turn up murky and lacklustre.

If this is where you're at right now, don't despair. Your aura will recover the minute you start making more mindful food choices. Be sure to stock up on fresh fruit and veg – of every colour of the rainbow – and you'll soon see this reflected in your own personal rainbow.

You should also make hydration a priority, drinking copious amounts of water throughout the day to keep your flow cleansed and super fresh.

If you've overindulged and you're feeling worse for wear, there is a way to combat your food/energy hangover. It's as simple as rebalancing your root chakra and, by extension, the physical first layer of your aura (the etheric body). A few drops of vetiver – an essential oil with an irresistible wood-smoky tang to it – applied straight to your belly button should be enough to set you on the road to recovery.

FLOOD YOUR AURA WITH LIGHT

When faced with a serious energy slump, never forget that your aura is made of light. So, if you're struggling to muster up the energy for that 3 p.m. meeting your boss just scheduled, take yourself out for a walk beforehand. Sunlight is a proven tonic for your aura. Under its warming, vitamin-D-rich influence, your aura will come alive.

ENERGY VAMPIRES: APPROACH WITH CAUTION

We've all got that friend, right? The "charming one" who's always getting into trouble, then expecting you to find a miracle fix... And don't expect them to ask how you're doing. Ever. Then there's your ex. You broke up months ago, but will they ever stop messaging you just to "check in"?

The takeaway? Energy vampires are all around us, and they come in many different guises.

Unlike their blood-sucking namesake, it's important to understand that energy vampires are not monsters. For the most part they're just really needy, draining the energies of those around them.

Some vamps may be completely unaware that this is their nature, while others are savvier. If you've got a conscious vamp on your hands, be warned: they'll keep taking advantage of your good nature until you put a stop to it, with a boundary they can't ignore.

That doesn't have to mean cutting them off completely. It can be as simple as limiting the time you spend in their company. It's perfectly acceptable to want to keep these people around, so long as you decide how much energy you can spare, without compromising your own well-being. Stay true to your inner voice, and stop saying "yes" when you're longing to say "no" to meet-ups, pleas for help and more.

You may even find that cutting back on time together is a saving grace for your relationship. When you do reconnect, you'll feel replenished and able to properly enjoy the vamp's company.

EXERCISE: PROTECT YOUR ENERGY

If distancing yourself from draining personalities won't work for you (maybe you're related to your vamp), don't worry. This meditation is tailor-made to get you through the most awkward social situations and lets you whip up a protective energy shield in minutes – a game-changer for empaths everywhere.

★ Close your eyes, bringing your attention to the breath.

★ Visualize your aura, surrounding you in a luminous cloud.

★ Picture a ray of dazzling white light, beaming down from the sky and into your aura. Watch as it floods your aura with its brilliance.

★ Call on the light: "Surround me, protect me, shield me from all the energies that would drain my light."

★ If you're in touch with spirit guides (via the celestial body), you can request their protection too.

★ Hold the meditation. Savour the feeling of how safe it is inside the pure white light until you're ready to open your eyes.

★ Whenever you're feeling anxious, call on this image and know your energy shield will come to your rescue.

ONCE IN A WHILE,
YOU DO ENCOUNTER BAD
ACQUAINTANCES, MEAN
PEOPLE, TOXIC AURAS.
DON'T LET THEM RENT
SPACE IN YOUR HEART
AND MIND.

RITA ZAHARA

FINDING YOUR FOREVER COLOUR

Auras exist in a state of constant flux, which is why it's important to check in on yours as often as you can, even as part of your daily routine.

Underneath it all, however, almost everyone possesses a dominant colour that never truly goes away. Instead it remains in our energy – in shade or lesser quantities – as the bedrock of our identity. Once you know which colour rules your energy, you'll find it easier to make lifestyle choices that chime with who you are – and that will strengthen your beautiful rainbow of colours. We'll explore this more fully later.

Try this fun, five-minute quiz to get to know yourself a little better.

QUIZ: WHICH COLOUR ARE YOU?

1. My dream job is:

A: Restaurant critic
B: Stunt person
C: Researcher
D: Vet

E: Artist

F: Teacher

G: Archaeologist

H: Freelance journalist

2. My ideal holiday destination is:

A: Sophisticated Rome

B: Untamed New Zealand

C: A Scottish Highlands hike

D: An English country cottage

E: Volunteering in Costa Rica

F: A dreamy Caribbean Island

G: Mysterious Cairo

H: A Himalayan retreat

3. In romantic relationships, I am:

A: Passionate

B: Adventurous

C: Deep

D: Nurturing

E: Caring and sensitive

F: Quick to fall in love

G: Dependable

H: Extremely giving

4. **My toxic trait is:**

   A: A fiery temper
   B: Doomscrolling
   C: Workaholic
   D: Jealousy
   E: Prone to low mood
   F: Unable to handle confrontation
   G: Tendency to meddle
   H: Not setting boundaries

5. **This Saturday, you'll find me:**

   A: Wining and dining my date
   B: Getting my adrenaline fix – I love
      extreme sports!
   C: Hosting a dinner party
   D: Pottering in the garden
   E: Painting with my dreamy watercolours
   F: Soaking in the bath
   G: Taking in some culture at the
      local museum
   H: On a solitary stroll through the woods

DECODING YOUR ANSWERS

Mostly As: You are a fiery red, with a passion for the finer things in life.

Mostly Bs: You are a zingy, thrill-seeking orange, with a zesty outlook on love and work.

Mostly Cs: You are a mellow yellow, with a serious thirst for knowledge and learning.

Mostly Ds: You are a green queen, loving, nurturing and at peace with the world.

Mostly Es: You are a sensitive, artistic blue, blessed with the gift of the gab.

Mostly Fs: You are a deeply empathetic violet, with a huge heart and psychic vision.

Mostly Gs: You're blessed to be a turquoise with an old soul and the Midas touch.

Mostly Hs: You are the rarest of things: a genuine, chameleonic crystal.

✦ HOME IS WHERE THE ART IS ✦

There's no denying the power of your surroundings to lift your mood. You know that feeling you get when you walk in the door after a long, hard day, shrug off your coat and your stresses? There's nothing like it. And what lightens your mood can't help but impact on your energy. So instead of following the latest trends, why not look to your auric colours for inspiration? That way, you'll end up with a shade that feels much more meaningful.

Here's how to become a dab hand at auric interior design.

★ Create a calming sanctuary, that replenishes your energy whenever you're home, by painting your walls in shades of your dominant colour. You can always play with subtle shades along with the odd splash of a complementary colour. For instance, nature-loving greens might pair a deep forest shade with pops of crisp mint and high notes of yellow. Adding layers of texture into the mix – a velvet sofa to vibe with matte walls and shiny ceramics – can also echo the multilayered structure of your aura.

- ★ Bonus points if your dominant colour matches with a major chakra. Surround yourself with this shade and the benefits will be twofold, nourishing both your aura *and* the chakra from which it flows.

- ★ If you're not 100 per cent sold on your chosen colour, try experimenting with accent pieces – try using a throw, cushion or candle in your auric colour. If you like how it makes you feel, you can always add more.

- ★ Embrace the trend for dip-dye candles and all things ombré, mimicking the beautifully fluid nature of your energy.

✦ PAINT YOUR WAY ✦ TO SUCCESS

Remember your aura can make things happen, so if you choose to align your auric decor with specific goals, you could find success starts flooding into your home and life.

For example, if you're struggling to stay productive while working from home, try filling your office with powerful pops of red. No other colour packs quite the same energizing punch. Or if you can't remember the last time you got a decent night's sleep, try splashing your bedroom walls with a peaceful shade of blue. Under its calming influence, you'll be able to properly unwind once your head touches the pillow.

THE POWER OF BALANCING SHADES

Just because a colour isn't your vibe doesn't mean you can't harness its best qualities for yourself. The first step to including a shade in your personal palette is adding it to your home. For instance:

★ Hot-headed reds wishing they could keep their emotions in check, will benefit from a dose of calming, centring green.

- ★ Single-minded yellows struggling to see things from any perspective other than their own, should immerse themselves in shades of violet – opening the way for a more empathetic connection with others.

- ★ Moody blues with their tendency to overthink every last detail should fill their homes with zesty orange, helping them to discover a new taste for adventure.

- ★ Empathetic crystals, in times when they're feeling burnt-out and overwhelmed by the vibes of others, should indulge in shades of sensual red to anchor them in the here and now – if only for a short while.

✦ AN AURA OF STYLE ✦

Never underestimate the power of a killer outfit. Clothes and make-up can transform your vibe beyond all recognition, as you've surely felt for yourself.

You know those days when you have your perfect look all planned out, then you try it on and it just feels *wrong*? That's the voice of your intuition, letting you know your chosen look is no match for where you're at energy-wise and will do you no favours on your date or in your meeting.

The secret to mindful dressing is to still your mind and let your intuition flow. No one knows your energy quite like you so trust in your inner voice and it will always steer you right.

On days when you feel there's something lacking, use magic flashes of colour to help you fake it till you make it. You don't have to dress from head to toe in a single shade, just one vibrant accessory can elevate your whole look.

COLOUR-POWERED DRESSING

- ★ If you're feeling anxious, clothe yourself in calming green to still your thoughts and quiet your mind.

- ★ If you want to feel like a strong, sensuous siren, a bold red lipstick can work wonders for your confidence. Match with your nails and sparkly statement jewellery.

- ★ Flashes of dynamic red are also great for the boardroom, letting your team know you're a force to be reckoned with.

- ★ If you're feeling fragile, sling on a smoky multicoloured labradorite pendant. With untold powers to soothe and protect your energy, it'll be the talisman you need to get through the toughest days.

GOOD VIBRATIONS, HARMONIOUS RELATIONS

Everyone you meet is sure to be vibing at their own unique frequency, from your passive-aggressive co-worker to your best friend. Whether their energy feels spiky or soothing, there's nothing you can do to change it, but that doesn't mean you can't try to lighten things up.

- **Be kind.** Random acts of kindness are good for the soul, setting your colours alight and creating the kind of energy that's impossible to keep to yourself. Sprinkle kindness freely among friends and colleagues, and you'll help lift the collective energy of your friendship group or workplace.

- **Channel your inner-violet.** A little empathy goes a long way when dealing with challenging personalities. Remembering that spiky auras are not born but made may help you to become the compassionate friend they need, letting them feel seen and heard in a way that everyone should.

- **Steer clear of triggering topics.** When in conversation with your prickly personality, avoid those dark spots in their energy and strive to reframe their critical thoughts in a positive light.

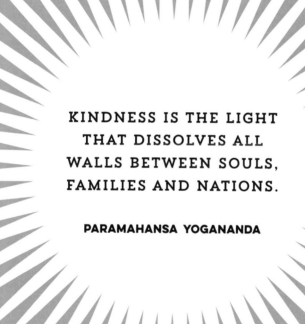

KINDNESS IS THE LIGHT
THAT DISSOLVES ALL
WALLS BETWEEN SOULS,
FAMILIES AND NATIONS.

PARAMAHANSA YOGANANDA

✦ THE DATING GAME ✦

The heart wants what the heart wants. And staying true to that is your surest way into the arms of "the one". When it comes to dating and your colours, there are no hard and fast rules. If someone's right for you then you'll find a way to make it work. If, on the other hand, the prospect of spending time in their company leaves you feeling edgy and uncomfortable, and you find yourself angsting over when – and if – you'll ever see their name appear in your DMs, then maybe it's time to take a step back. Once again, it's a question of learning to lean into your natural intuitions.

PASSIONATE REDS

Kiss: Reds, oranges and yellows
Marry: Greens and violets
Swipe left: Blues, turquoises and crystals

ARDENT YELLOWS

Kiss: Reds, oranges and violets
Marry: Yellows and blues
Swipe left: Greens

SENSITIVE BLUES

Kiss: Blues
Marry: Yellows, violets and crystals
Swipe left: Reds and greens

LOVING GREENS

Kiss: Crystals
Marry: Reds, oranges, turquoises and violets
Swipe left: Yellows and blues

DEVOTED TURQUOISES

Kiss: Blues
Marry: Violets and crystals
Swipe left: Reds

TRUE-HEARTED VIOLETS

Kiss: Crystals
Marry: Reds, greens, blues and violets
Swipe left: Oranges

ADVENTUROUS ORANGES

Kiss: Reds and yellows
Marry: Oranges and greens
Swipe left: Violets and crystals

INTENSE CRYSTALS

Kiss: Crystals
Marry: Blues and violets
Swipe left: Reds, oranges and greens

KEEP THE LOVE ALIVE

Never forget that the lush green heart chakra is what lets us lavish love on our romantic partners and receive love in return. When this chakra closes, the astral body (layer four of our aura) can't possibly function as it should. Rather than beaming out into the world in search of new connections, shining love and light on everyone it touches, it shrinks down to almost nothing.

To avoid this disastrous energy situation, you need to keep your heart chakra open and overflowing with love, via:

* Meditation, while chanting the mantra of "yam" – the secret sound that speaks straight to the heart chakra.

* Draping yourself in green clothing.

* Bathing with any of the following essential oils: eucalyptus, geranium, jasmine, rose or ylang ylang. Or if you prefer, scent the air using a diffuser.

* Surrounding yourself with gorgeous green crystals: aventurine, malachite and jade.

✦ TIME FOR A CLEANSE ✦

No matter how carefully you guard your aura, it's impossible to rid yourself of negative vibes completely. We're exposed to them out in the world, every single day.

Habit energy – when we find ourselves caught up in endless loops of unhelpful thought that just don't serve us – also has a part to play. So if you ever find yourself stuck, in a stagnant situation where nothing seems to shift, then you're likely a victim of pesky habit energy, building up over time.

Maybe you're suffering from low mood, feeling like you have the whole world weighing on your shoulders, and you no longer have the headspace for the things that bring you joy. All of these are red flags, letting you know it's time for an auric cleanse, to rid yourself of everything that's dragging you down.

Armed with the following exercises, there's no need for you to be carrying these negative energies around a moment longer. Their time living rent-free in your energy ends now.

EXERCISE: SCAN, CLEANSE, REPEAT

Use this visualization for self-care at the end of each long week, or whenever you feel the need.

★ Settle down in your space, sitting comfortably or lying on a heap of cosy pillows. Place one hand on your heart and the other on your tummy. Inhale, drawing the breath deep into your heart and down through your belly. Feel your hands rise and fall in a calming cycle.

★ Let your eyes close. Visualize your auric bubble taking shape around your body.

★ Turn your attention to the outer layer. Does it have the pure white shimmer you'd expect? Or is it marred by cloudy colours and dark patches? Scan the surface with your breath.

★ Focus on any stains and watch them fade as your breath works like a cleansing filter to melt them away.

★ With every breath, feel your outer layer swell, aglow with strength and health.

★ Now explore deeper with your cleansing breath. Ask your aura to reveal itself: "Show me the layers where my light shines dim, the colours I need to heal."

★ Breathe and trust the layers you seek will appear in whatever guise is right for you. Don't be surprised if that's a sound or a hunch rather than visual. Be ready to repeat your mantra until you see a fresh set of colours materialize.

★ Focus your healing breath and feel the taint of these unwanted energies lift with each inhale, and know they'll be carried away on your next exhale.

★ Repeat these steps for as long as new colours appear in your mind's eye.

★ Thank mother earth for absorbing the negative vibes and emerge from your visualization – feeling blissfully cleansed and light.

✦ CRYSTAL POWER ✦

To give your aura an extra lift, you may wish to explore the magic world of crystals. These pocket treasures are all vibing at their own frequencies – just like us. Simply pop one under your pillow or carry it with you during the day, and you'll begin to feel the benefits.

POCKET HEROES AND CRYSTAL REMEDIES

- ★ When life's thrown you a curveball, leaving your auric layers and chakras completely out of sync, reach for a hunk of clear quartz. There's no better way to restore the natural balance of your subtle body.

- ★ Nothing soothes your emotional body like a dreamy piece of turquoise larimar.

- ★ Want to transform your negative vibes into something beautiful? Then amethyst is your best friend.

- ★ Give yourself an energy glow-up, banishing trapped vibes from your flow with dazzling sunstone.

* Tears in your aura (caused by low self-esteem or the harsh energies of others) equal an energy emergency. Labradorite is the saviour you need to repair them.

* Named after the mysterious moon goddess Selene, selenite is powered by pure white light, which makes it the queen of cleansing crystals.

EXERCISE: A SELENITE CLEANSE

* Hold the crystal selenite "wand" in your hands and find a comfortable sitting position. Focus on your breathing until your mind feels quiet.

* Call on the wand in your hands: "Selene, please take the impurities from my energy, and replace them with your own white and loving light."

* Comb through your aura with the crystal, taking care to sweep it every which way to cover the whole of your energy field.

* Picture the dull specks of energy as you dust them off your aura and the pure white light pouring in to take its place.

* Continue with your mantra and your cleanse until you feel refreshed.

OTHER WAYS TO CLEANSE AND HEAL

COMFORT IN SOUND

We can hear sounds and even feel them in our physical bodies. And their effect on our subtle body is just as strong. Whenever your energy is not vibing at its usual frequency, sound can be the perfect tonic. Find one that speaks to your soul.

It could be a special piece of music that unlocks your emotions or creates internal calm, or sounds of the natural world. Perhaps it's a chanted mantra, a tuning fork or a set of singing bowls.

SMUDGE YOUR WAY TO CLARITY

Smudging – the burning of sacred herbs – is used to smoke negative energies from your auric field. White sage is ideal, but cedar, garden sage, juniper, rosemary or lavender can create a similar effect.

Bundle them together in a chunky wand, but be careful when you light it as it can create a powerful flame. Blow it out, leaving the end to smoke, then waft along the length of your body in all directions, asking mother earth to take negative energies from your flow. Thank her gracefully when finished.

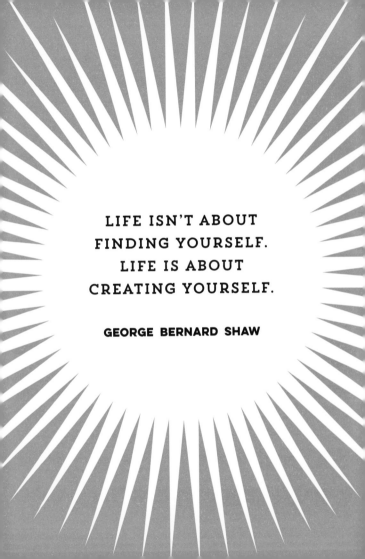

✦ CONCLUSION ✦

The end of *The Little Book of Auras* marks a thrilling new chapter for you. Your future as a radiant, spiritually-aware being is only just beginning, like a story yet to be written. And now, armed with everything you've learned, you're ready to reclaim the narrative. After all, there's no more powerful way to attract the future of your dreams than by intentionally setting the frequency of your vibe.

The chapters you've read are information-heavy, taking you deep inside your aura's intricate structure. Even if you've only just begun to sense the beauteous colours of your aura, you should feel proud of how far you've come.

If you take one thing from this book, let it be an unshakeable faith in your own abilities. You are so much more than what the eye can see. That blossoming intuition of yours, the one we've been nurturing with mantras and meditation, has been with you all along. The power to manifest your dreams, radiating love and light wherever you go in this world, is in your hands. Never be afraid to let your colours shine.

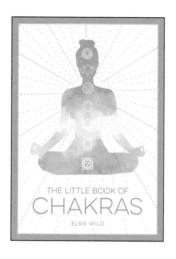

THE LITTLE BOOK OF CHAKRAS
Elsie Wild

Paperback • ISBN: 978-1-78783-685-3

Chakras are your body's spiritual centres of healing energy. This beginner's guide explains the seven major chakras and how to channel their energy for optimum health. Exploring each chakra's mental and physical aspects, the book shows how diet, yoga and meditation, along with crystals and essential oils, can bring balance to your daily life.

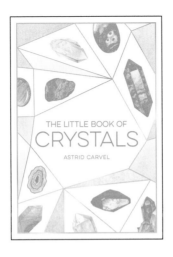

THE LITTLE BOOK OF CRYSTALS

Astrid Carvel

Paperback • ISBN: 978-1-78685-959-4

Learn how to select and maintain your crystals as well as basic techniques for crystal meditation, balancing chakras and simple ways to bring harmony to mind, body and spirit with these natural treasures. Discover over 50 crystals, their unique properties and how to make use of their power in everyday life. There is a crystal for every occasion.

Have you enjoyed this book?
If so, find us on Facebook at Summersdale
Publishers, on Twitter/X at @Summersdale and
on Instagram and TikTok at @summersdalebooks
and get in touch. We'd love to hear from you!

www.summersdale.com

Image credits